The Chapter on Music
in
JOHANNES THOMAS FREIG'S
PAEDAGOGUS

MUSICOLOGICAL STUDIES & DOCUMENTS

The Chapter on Music
in
JOHANNES THOMAS FREIG'S PAEDAGOGUS

PUBLICATIONS OF THE
AMERICAN INSTITUTE OF MUSICOLOGY
ARMEN CARAPETYAN
DIRECTOR

MUSICOLOGICAL STUDIES & DOCUMENTS

38

JOHANNES THOMAS FREIG

(1543-1583)

PAEDAGOGUS

1582

THE CHAPTER ON MUSIC

Translated and Edited
with an
Introduction
by
JEREMY YUDKIN

AMERICAN INSTITUTE OF MUSICOLOGY
HÄNSSLER-VERLAG
1983
68.738

Hänssler-Verlag, D 7303 Neuhausen-Stuttgart.
Order-No. 68.738
ISBN 3-7751-0657-X

CONTENTS

IOAN. THOMÆ FREIGII I. V. D.

PAEDAGOGVS.

HOC EST, LIBELLVS OSTENDENS QVA RATIONE PRIMA ARTIVM INItia pueris quàm facillimè tradi possint.

BASILEÆ,
PER SEBASTIANVM HENRICPETRI

INTRODUCTION

The ability fully to understand an earlier era in music is, to a large extent, dependent upon the availability of original source material. Reliance upon secondary sources, in a field as diverse and disparate as music, is, at best, hazardous. In his *Fourscore Classics of Music Literature,* published in 1957, Gustave Reese commented on the importance of consulting original sources, and, as a general as well as a specific stimulus, compiled a selective list of books which were unavailable in English translation and which he believed were relevant to a fuller comprehension of the periods they represented.

Since that time many more books have been made available in facsimile or modern editions, and some in English translation. But there remains a large number of books (some even on Reese's list) that have yet to be translated. And of these some of the most important are in Latin.

It may not be superfluous here to remind ourselves of the pervasiveness of Latin in the history of Western culture. For hundreds of years Latin was the only language, and for hundreds more the primary language, of Western scholars. During the Renaissance, important books in the vernacular (for example Virdung's *Musica getutscht,* 1511, or Machiavelli's *Il Principe,* 1532) were important partly because they were early exceptions to this general rule. And even in the practical and egalitarian eighteenth century, great writers like Fux (*Gradus ad Parnassum,* 1725) and Blumenbach (*De generis humani varietate nativa,* 1775) chose to publish their work in Latin, as the international and traditional language of scholarship.

Apart from the major musical treatises, many of which can now be found in English, there are numerous books which were not revolutionary, or notable as musical milestones, which can nevertheless contribute to our overall understanding of the musical life or consciousness of earlier times.

One such class of book that has been investigated very little in the field of musicology is the schoolbook. From it we may catch a glimpse of the musical background not just of the composers and practical musicians, but also of the educated public of the time.

My choice of this particular work for translation was determined by several factors. First, I was fortunate enough to have access to an original copy of the first edition. Secondly, the extensive music chapter (the longest in the book) seemed to suggest that the author had more than a cursory interest in the subject. And thirdly, hardly any modern research has been done on Freig, or his writings on music,[1] and, so far as I can determine,[2] nobody has attempted to translate any part of the *Paedagogus.*

Johannes Thomas Freig, son of the lawyer and humanist scholar, Nicolaus Freig, was born in 1543 in Freiburg-im-Breisgau in Southern Germany. He received his education in Freiburg, where Glarean was one of his teachers. After graduating he began teaching dialectic and Latin grammar but soon turned to law. In 1567 he went to Basel where he taught rhetoric, but continued his legal studies, receiving his doctorate in 1568. There he met Pierre de La Ramée (Ramus), who had fled to Germany from the religious wars which were raging at that time in France. La Ramée was an extremely influential and controversial figure in the sixteenth century,[3] and in the two years that he spent at Basel he managed to make a deep and lasting impression on Freig.

From that time on, Freig was an enthusiastic disciple of Ramist philosophy, studying dialectic, rhetoric, philosophy, jurisprudence and mathematics. In 1570 he returned to Freiburg as Professor of

[1]There are short entries in Eitner, Fétis and the new Gerber; and Walter Thoene in *Friedrich Beurhaus und seine Musiktraktate,* 1959, gives some brief comments on Freig. The *Paedagogus* is mentioned in Nan Cooke Carpenter, *Music in the Medieval and Renaissance Unversities, 1958.*

[2]See Appendix II.

[3]For further reading on La Ramée, and the philosophical divergences between the Ramists and Aristotelians, see F.P. Graves: *Peter Ramus and the Educational Reformation of the 16th Century,* 1912; and studies by N.E. Nelson, and W.J. Ong.

Dialectic, and in 1571 and 1573 was also appointed to the Professorships of Ethics and Philosophy. After La Ramée's death in 1572 during the St. Bartholemew's Day massacre, Freig devoted much of his time to editing and publishing the works and teachings of his mentor.[4] Ramist philosophy, however, was by no means universally accepted among academics at that time, and after several confrontations with the establishment at Freiburg, in 1575 Freig went back to Basel, where he made a living as an editor and worked on his own publications.

In 1576 he was appointed rector to the college at Altdorf, where he taught philosophy, jurisprudence and philology, and continued his literary work. In time, however, his loyalty to La Ramée became the cause of further conflict, and in 1582 he resigned his post and returned to Basel.

There he resumed his position as editor at the Henricpetri printing shop, but the plague took his three children that same year, and he himself died on the 16th of January, 1583, at the age of 39.

During his life Freig published many books — on Classical authors, logic, history, physics, Greek and Latin grammar, geometry, ethics and law — demonstrating an eclectic scholarship so typical of sixteenth-century humanism. The *Paedagogus* alone contains chapters on twenty-three different subjects, of which music is but one, and it is with this in mind that we must consider the content and presentation of the musical material in the book.

The *Paedagogus* is a schoolbook — not a treatise or a manual. In the dedication, which was written by Freig's two sons, it is stressed that the book is intended to serve only as an introduction to the various subjects, and the subtitle of the book itself is a disclaimer of definitive treatment.

[4]One of these books was the *P. Rami professio regia,* published in 1576. Fétis is in error when he states: "il est divisé en sept parties, dont une est relative à la musique." In fact the seven parts are CICERONIANUS, GRAMMATICA, RHETORICA, DIALECTICA, ARITHMETICA, PHYSICA, ETHICA.

Nonetheless, the music chapter is in fact quite detailed. We learn from the suggested timetable at the beginning of the book that, beginning in the second year, a fair amount of time was to be spent in the study of music; and by the fourth year the amount of time recommended for devotion to music is greater than that for any other single subject.[5]

In his list of suggested reading, Freig says that he has taken his musical precepts from Glarean, and in fact the chapter on music is based to a large extent on the *Dodecachordon,* which was published in 1547. Most of Glarean's extensive treatise, however, could obviously not be included in a short chapter of this kind, and it is instructive to see what has been omitted, and what was considered fundamental enough for inclusion.

Freig deals with solmisation syllables, note lengths, rests, ligatures and clefs; he also discusses the intervals, the tetrachord, mutation, mensuration, and the modes. He does not include any of the speculative or ethical aspects of music that Glarean discusses. He does not indulge in the lengthy (and often fascinating) digressions about historical perspectives, contemporary personalities, and musical criticism that Glarean allows himself. And, apart from two or three brief comments, there is no discussion of polyphonic music, and there are no polyphonic musical examples, which form such an important part of Glarean's book.

However, even when dealing with areas covered by Glarean, Freig's chapter on music is by no means a digest of the *Dodecachordon.* Apart from two of the Horatian odes and the song to illustrate the intervals, all of Freig's musical examples, copious and apposite, are new. The arrangement and treatment of the subject matter is entirely his own, and some of the ideas (for example the discussion of musical artifice) are not in Glarean at all.

[5]In *The Theory and Practice of Protestant School Music As Seen Through the Collection of Abraham Ursinus (c. 1600),* (Ph.D. dissertation, University of Rochester, Eastman School of Music, 1962), Ernest Livingstone has shown that music was a central, indeed an integral, part of the school curriculum.

Comparison of the musical examples reveals a striking difference between the two books. Many of Freig's examples are secular, whereas almost all of Glarean's are sacred music. In the *Dodecachordon* Glarean continually stresses the religious importance of music and makes apologies for introducing his few secular compositions, whereas Freig seems perfectly at ease with the more modern German "Lieder," or French "chansons." For most of the remainder of his examples Freig turns, not to the great composers of the previous generation, as Glarean had done, but to Alexander Utendal's *Penitential Psalms,* which had been published not long before, and were "fitted to the twelve modes of the *Dodecachordon.*"

Another important difference lies in the format of the two books. The *Paedagogus* is cast in the question and answer form common to early schoolbooks, as opposed to the discursive style used by Glarean. This allows Freig a simplicity and directness in the presentation of his material that is more suitable for his task.

Perhaps the point of primary interest in the chapter on music is the discussion of the modes. Although Glarean's theory of the twelve modes had been established many years before, and was reestablished or reiterated by such important theorists as Zarlino, Vincenzo Galilei and Thomas Morley, it was by no means universally accepted in the musical world of the late sixteenth century. As late as 1609 John Dowland published his translation of Ornithoparcus, which contained the standard eight modes. The *Micrologus* was of course written nearly a hundred years earlier, but Dowland's intention of reestablishing the traditional formulae was clear.

Sixteenth-century schoolbooks were particularly slow to accept Glarean's theory. According to Thoene,[6] the first schoolbook to treat of twelve modes was the *Musicae practicae elementa* of Gallus Dressler, published in 1571. But there were many texts, both before and after Freig, that retained the standard grouping.

[6]Op. cit.

In 1580 the second edition of the *Erotematum musicae* by Friedrich Beurhaus (Beurhusius) appeared, with a preface by Freig. Beurhaus was a colleague and fellow adherent to the philosophy of La Ramée, and Freig's preface is friendly but critical. His major concern is that the book mentions only eight modes and does not properly explain their quality and nature. He recommends the inclusion of an analysis of the *Penitential Psalms* of Utendal, together with a detailed discussion of the twelve modes.[7]

This preface also gives us an interesting insight into Freig's own relationship with the modal theory of Glarean. Towards the end he writes:

> Atque memini illius temporis, quo Glareanum de hac re docentem, atque contra antagonistas suos . . . . de hac re copiose ac ardenter differentem puer audivi: sed haec tum ob aetatis fragile iudicium a me parum intellecta, atque postea ob alia studia, ad quae magis ferebat natura, intermissa, nunc me summa poenitentia afficiunt. [p. 7]
>
> And I remember when as a boy I heard Glarean lecturing thoroughly, enthusiastically and argumentatively against his opponents . . . . on this subject. But I understood little of it at that time because my intellect was youthful and undeveloped, and later because other studies, to which my nature was more inclined, intervened — both of which I now very much regret.

We can get a fairly accurate picture of the timing of Freig's conversion by an examination of Book Seven ("De sono et musica") of his *Quaestiones physicae,* for there a table clearly shows eight modes, four authentic and four plagal, with Ionian even given as an alternative name for Lydian. The book was published in 1579. By February of 1580 Freig was criticizing Beurhaus in his prefatory letter. And two and a half years later the *Paedagogus* appeared with its detailed exposition of Glarean's theory.

[7]In the epilogue Beurhaus says that he will correct his book in accordance with the views of his critics, but later editions of the *Erotematum* (1585 and 1591) remained unchanged. The *Musicae rudimenta* of Beurhaus, printed in 1581, also contains an explanation of only eight modes.

In describing the qualities of the modes, Freig generally harks back to the oft-iterated quotations from Classical authors.[8] In so doing, of course, he is completely in tune with the tenor of the times, when a primary concern was the establishment of a direct link between the ancient (Classical) and modern eras, forming a bridge over the intervening years, when "honestae disciplinae una cum bonis litteris plusque sopitae iacebant" (honorable study and fine scholarship were lying asleep).[9] The books on music throughout the sixteenth century echo with the juxtaposition of the words "ancient" and "modern."[10] And Glarean states firmly in his preface to the *Dodecachordon:*

> Constat igitur non esse novam rem hanc nostram de XII modis assertionem, sed probam antiquitatis instaurationem.

> Therefore it is established that this declaration of mine about the twelve modes is not a new idea, but a true revival of antiquity.

Often, however, an editorial comment or opinion by Freig shows that his reiteration of literary commonplaces by no means precludes originality of treatment. Some of the descriptions of modal affect seem to be his own, or at least are dependent neither upon Classical antecedent nor upon Glarean.

This introduction to music was written by a man of more than ordinary dedication to his subject; and his "little book" appeared at an important point in the history of the art, when change was rapid, and old theories, not yet firmly established, were already being challenged by new ideas and practices.

[8]By 1597 Morley already considered this unnecessary. In his *A Plaine and Easie Introduction to Practicall Musicke,* (p. 147) he says, "Every key hath a peculiar ayre proper unto it selfe," but he dispenses with the Classical allusions.

[9]*Dodecachordon* I, xvi, 43.

[10]Nicolo Vincenzo. *L'Antica Musica ridotta alla moderna prattica.* 1555.
Vincenzo Galilei. *Dialogo della musica antica e della moderna.* 1581
Girolamo Mei. *Discorso sopra la musica antica e moderna.* 1602.

The opening definition dispenses immediately with the theoretical reasonings that Glarean, Zarlino and others thought obligatory, and states simply:

Quid est Musica?
Est ars bene canendi.[11]
(What is Music?
It is the art of singing well).

The appended Horatian settings, though part of a long (especially German) tradition, look forward to a new age of word consciousness and natural declamation of text. Though based firmly on the theory and practice of one era, Freig's music chapter stands clearly on the threshold of another.

[11]Pierre de la Ramée had defined all the arts similarly: Arithmetica est ars bene numerandi. Ethica est ars bene vivendi. etc.

SOME NOTES ON THE TRANSLATION

The primary goal of a translator should be transparency. The author's original ideas must be illuminated as much and distorted as little as possible by the new language. This is important for a work of fiction, but it is even more important for a work of information.

My purpose has been to allow other students of music access to a book they might otherwise have been unable to read, and I have therefore resisted every temptation to paraphase, adapt, polish or otherwise "improve" the original. I have, of course, tried to make the English as fluent and readable as possible, but where necessary I have sacrificed elegance for accuracy.

There were certain specific problems that I encountered while working on the translation that were a result of the subtle but critical changes that have occured in the meaning of some technical musical terms in the course of the last four hundred years. Thus "mensura"does not mean "measure" in the sense that we now use the word, and we therefore cannot translate it that way (though in 1609 Dowland could); it means "a system of measuring" or (as I have translated it) "mensuration."

Consistency in the original would sometimes have helped, but Freig is not consistent. So "voces," normally used to describe the solmisation syllables (and translated"syllables"), is twice used in the more modern sense to refer to the different parts of a polyphonic composition, and there I have used the English word "voices."

"Clavis" ("a key") means the line or space on the staff that designates the position of a note, and also (by transference) the letter name of the note. Here I have simply used the word "key", as any other translation would have rendered much of the surrounding material unintelligible. There seems little danger of ambiguity in context.

There are some occasional inaccuracies, inconsistencies or misprints in the text and these I have indicated in the footnotes.

I have also used footnotes fairly extensively to comment on certain passages, to point out clear parallels with or divergences from Glarean's text, to explain Classical allusions, and to translate Greek words where they are not immediately translated in the text.[1]

I have restored all "Latinised" proper names to their original form, and have reproduced all the musical examples from the text.

[1]I have retained the distinction between the use of Greek or Latin characters for Greek words in accordance with the original.

THE PAEDAGOGUS

JOHANNES THOMAS FREIG

Doctor of ecclesiastical & civil law[1]

THE INSTRUCTOR — A LITTLE BOOK SHOWING HOW THE FIRST STEPS IN THE ARTS CAN BE VERY EASILY TAUGHT TO YOUNG STUDENTS.

PRINTED AT BASEL
by
SEBASTIAN HENRICPETRI[2]

To a man most famous for his nobility, and outstanding in sagacity, Lord Johannes Martin Amelius,[3] *most worthy Chancellor of the most illustrious princes, the Margrafs of Hochburg, greetings and salutations, and may your own Lord protect you.*

[1] The Latin abbreviation is I. V. D. or Juris Utriusque Doctor, an honorific explained by the title of another of Freig's books: *Partitiones* juris utriusque; *hoc est omnium* juris tam civilis quam canonici *materiarum, in tabulas... digestio....* (A treatise of both kinds of law... both civil and ecclesiastical....)

[2] This printing shop had been started two generations earlier by Adam Petri in 1490. From 1527 it was owned by his son, Heinrich Petri, who became one of the most important printers of his time in the fields of medicine, astronomy and mathematics. In 1556 Heinrich Petri was raised to the rank of nobleman by Karl V and entitled to use the form Henric-petri. At his death in 1579, this privilege, together with the printing shop, passed to his sons Sebastian and Sixtus who ran the shop until 1627.

[3] Martin A. Amelius, 1526-1592, attended the university of Freiburg where he studied law. Later he went to Vienna where he obtained a doctorate and was made a nobleman by King Ferdinand. On his return in 1554 he was appointed Chancellor to the Margraf Karl II of Baden-Durlach, and from 1556 lived at Pforzheim.

Since these introductions to the arts, most noble and honorable sir, which our father, *Johannes Thomas Freig,* had privately communicated to us, were so popular with young students that they were talked about by many of them with eagerness and enthusiasm, we decided to have them printed, so that what had previously been circulated only in private could now be publicly available. Our father had no other intention in writing these introductions than to accustom us to the simple jargon of the arts, and enable us to understand and commit to memory a vocabulary put together and arranged into a legitimate method. For he does not have so light an estimation of the arts as to believe he could make full-fledged philosophers, doctors or lawyers out of us from these simple statements. But he thought that by learning these elementary words and their meanings we could at least stammer along in philosophy, medicine or law, so that although at first we might learn slowly and inaccurately, later we could become quicker and more thorough, with the result that when we were older we could advance more easily to a study of the subjects in their entirety and not be hindered or tripped by roughnesses in the path. For he knows that old saying: ἀρχη ἡμισυ παντος ,[4] and that line in the poet:

> The task is halfway done
> By him who has well begun.[5]

The reason, most distinguished Sir, for our wanting to publish these simple introductions under your name was that our father very often used to mention how you and he were born in the same town, and how you and our ancestors were acquainted. For Freiburg, that city of the ancient Harelungi (who were succeeded

[4] "The beginning is half of the whole". Ancient proverb. (v. Hesiod, *Works and Days,* 40. Aristotle, *Nicomachean Ethics* I, vii. Lucian, *Hermotimus*, 3. etc.)

[5] Dimidium facti, qui bene cepit, habet, Horace, *Epistles* I, ii, 40.

by the Brisgoi, who took their name from Mount Breisach) that city made famous by Zasius,[6] was a common birthplace for both you and our father. And he taught us how his father, *Nicolaus Freig*[7] (who was born nearby in Mark, in the village of Schalbach) and his relatives, and your Honor, had been acquainted because you were neighbors — a relationship that in the playwright's work is considered by no means low on the scale of friendship.[8]

So may your Honor accept these simple introductions and these first examples of our studies in the most favorable light; and whenever an occasion should arise for us to travel (as if by the ancient right of return)[9] to Mark, our grandfather's birthplace, may your Honor aid us with his favor and goodwill. We in our turn, together with our father, pledge our full allegiance and gratitude. May the *great and good God above* long protect and keep you safe at Mark.

Dated the 1st of September in the year of our Lord 1582 at Basel.

Your Honor's most devoted servants,

Johannes Thomas and
Johannes Oswald
Freig.

[6]Ulrich Zasius, 1461-1536. One of the most renowned humanists and scholars of Germany in his time. His teaching of the law earned him a reputation both at home and abroad, and his books on jurisprudence were read and respected as far afield as Padua. Nicolaus Freig, the father of Johannes Thomas, was a pupil of Zasius, and helped him achieve even wider recognition after his death through further editions of his works.

[7]Nicolaus Freig, ?-1552. The son of a wealthy landowner, he attended Freiburg university. He was a student of the law, and a pupil and ardent admirer of Ulrich Zasius. He was active as a lawyer in Rappolstein and at the court in Ensisheim, before being appointed legal representative for the town of Freiburg. In 1544 he moved to a similar appointment in Ulm, where he died in 1552.

[8]Freig refers here to "Comicus" (the comic poet), possibly meaning Terence, the second-century Latin playwright referred to by Glarean in his dedication.

[9]Postliminium - the ancient privilege by which Roman citizens were entitled to return to their full privileges and possessions after being away at war.

DIVISION OF THE ARTS

- The Arts
  - Academic
    - Oratory
      - Unmetred
        - Pure Grammar
        - Embellished, which is Rhetoric
      - Metred, which is Poetry
    - Logic
  - Gratifying to the senses
    - Mathematics
      - Arithmetic
        - Architecture
        - Weights & Measures
        - Mechanics
      - Geometry
    - Physics
      - Music
      - Astronomy
      - Geography
      - Medicine
    - Ethics
      - Economics
      - Politics
      - The study of antiquity
      - The study of foreign lands
      - Polemics
      - History
      - Jurisprudence
      - Theology

How are the liberal arts divided?

Into academic subjects, and subjects that are gratifying to the senses. At least, that is how Aristotle distinguishes them.

How many of the former are there?

Four: Grammar, Rhetoric, Poetry and Logic.

And of the latter?

Three: Mathematics, Physics and Ethics.

How many kinds of Mathematics are there?

Two: Arithmetic and Geometry. Geometry is subdivided into Weights and Measures, Architecture and Mechanics.

And which subjects come under Physics?

Music, Astronomy, Geography and Medicine.

And which come under Ethics?

Economics, Politics, The Study of Foreign Lands, the Study of Antiquity, Polemics, History and Jurisprudence.

Advice to young students

In this "Instructor" of ours we have tried to show what steps students can take in order to arrive at some προγνωσιν or foreknowledge of the arts. We have therefore thought it worthwhile to show by what method and at what rate of progress pupils should be taught, as well as what books they should read, once they have mastered these initial steps, so that they can achieve a fuller γνωσιν or understanding of the arts. So we begin with these few words:

I. The Method and Rate of Progress in this "Instructor".

First year

1. Students should learn the Latin alphabet.
2. They should learn how to join syllables together, by learning some vocabulary and examples of declensions and conjugations.

3. They should learn to read, using the same vocabulary and grammar.
4. At the same time they should learn how to write.
5. One day a week they should also learn how to paint. They should draw a foot, a hand, a head, shoes, socks, or a horse, or something similar that they could copy.

Second year

Little by little students should learn the following:

On Mondays, Tuesdays and Wednesdays, at	9 a.m.	Holy Scriptures, with declensions and conjugations.
	12 p.m.	Music.
	4 p.m.	Actual conversations, with declensions and conjugations. Also some vocabulary.
On Thursdays, at	9 a.m.	Arithmetic, each according to his ability.
	4 p.m.	The Epistles of Cicero. A discussion of them should be held, according to each student's ability.
On Saturdays, at	9 a.m.	They should write in Latin, German and Greek, and learn an elegant hand.
	12 p.m.	They should read the Scriptures aloud in German, and learn to read them in Greek also.
	4 p.m.	They should learn Catechism.

One day a week they should practise their painting.

Third year

Students should learn the same as for the second year, and practise it; as well as improving their Latin syntax and Greek grammar.

Fourth year

Students should practise the following:

On Mondays, Tuesdays, and Wednesdays, at	9 a.m.	On alternate weeks, they should listen to	The poets: Virgil, Ovid, Terence, Horace & Juvenal The historians: Justin, Caesar, etc.
	12 p.m.	Music.	
	4 p.m.	A summary of all the other subjects.	
On Thursdays, at	9 a.m.	Arithmetic & Geometry.	
	12 p.m.	Music.	
	4 p.m.	The Epistles of Cicero.	
On Fridays, at	8 a.m.	The same as Monday, Tuesday and Wednesday.	
	12 p.m.	Music.	
	4 p.m.	The Epistles of Cicero.	
On Saturdays, at	8 a.m.	Greek grammar and the Scriptures in Greek.	
	12 p.m.	Hebrew grammar, and the Hebrew Scriptures.	
	4 p.m.	Catechism, the Gospel according to St. Matthew, and the Epistles of St. Paul.	

At dinner also, on	Saturday.	They should read some discussion of the Scriptures in Latin, or German.
	Sunday.	The New and the Old Testament.

The times can be changed at the discretion of the teacher, and in choosing books and determining the rate of progress the ability of the individual student must be taken into account.

II. What books should be read, and in what order?

[There follows a long list of books for every subject heading in the "Paedagogus", and under *Music* Freig recommends:]

. . . Boethius,[1] and the *Dodecachordon* of Glarean. We have taken our precepts from Glarean, though many of the examples are from the works of Utendal.

[After the book list there is an epigram by Pantaleon,[2] a short poem in hexameter verse in praise of Freig, describing some of his previous books and lauding this particular effort of his, which, while it brings no great glory, yet will be an important and useful achievement for the benefit of young people.

There follows, before the main body of the book, a Latin version of Psalm 37, the psalm that begins:

> Fret not thyself because of evil-doers, neither be thou envious against the workers of iniquity.
>
> For they shall be cut down like the grass, and wither as the green herb.
>
> Trust in the Lord, and do good; so shalt thou dwell in the land, and verily thou shalt be fed.
>
> (From the King James translation).]

[1]It is worthy of note that in 1546 the Henricpetri establishment at Basel printed the complete works of Boethius (*Anitii Manlii Severini Boetii, . . . opera quae extant omnia*) with a preface by Glarean, who also edited the sections on music and arithmetic. A second edition appeared in 1570. My references are to this latter edition.

[2]Heinrich P. Pantaleon, 1522-1595. German scholar and historian. His most important work was the *Prosopographia heroum atque illustrium virorum totius Germaniae* . . . , Basel, 1565-1566, a complete history of Germany from prehistoric times, in the form of biographies of its famous men.

[The *Paedagogus* itself consists of the following chapters, given in order:

	page numbers	*number of pages*
Latin grammar	1- 18	18
Greek grammar	19- 50	32
Hebrew grammar	51- 80	30
French conversation	81-124	44
Rhetoric	125-130	6
Poetry	131-132	2
Logic	133-143	11
Arithmetic	144-156	13
Music	157-217	61
Geometry	218-224	7
Weights & Measures	225-247	23
Architecture	247-263	17
Mechanics	264-268	5
Physics	269-286	18
Ethics	287-290	4
Economics	290-295	6
Study of foreign lands	295-297	3
Study of antiquity	297-303	7
Polemics	304-310	7
History	310-313	4
Jurisprudence	313-317	5
Rudiments of the Law	317-341	25
Medicine	342-366	25]

I. Scale of Guido of Arezzo.

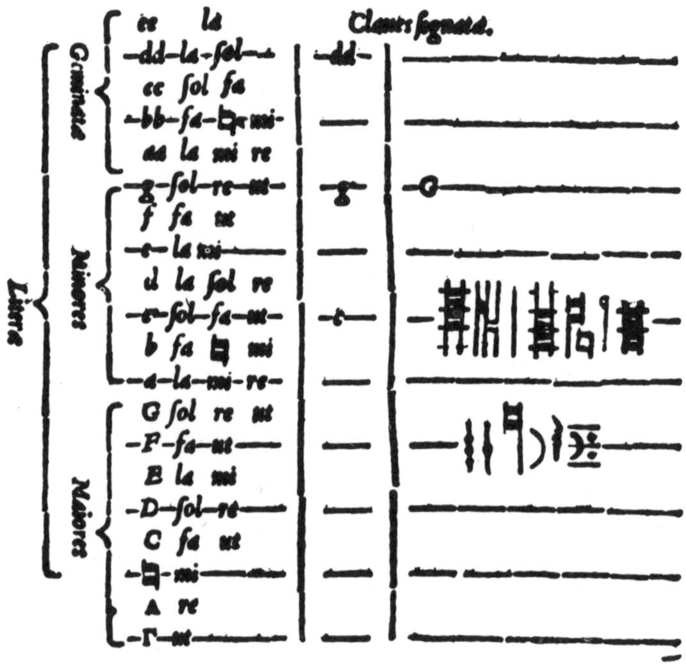

II. Names of Syllables.

Syllables
- Upper
  - La
  - Sol
  - Fa
- Lower
  - Mi
  - Re
  - Ut

III. Signs.

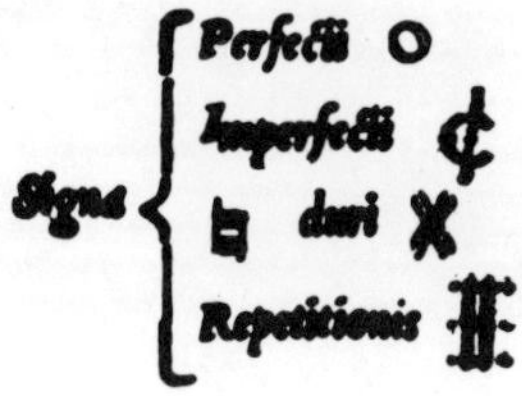

IV. Duration of Notes and Rests.

V. Ligatures.

VI. Scale, or Progression of Syllables.

Progression of six syllables, with alternate intervals of thirds and fourths:

MUSIC

What is Music?

It is the art of singing well. Its subject is proportioned sound. A former student of ours, Conrad Stuber,[1] has written a short book about this, but he has not yet had it printed. We shall follow in his tracks.

How is the chapter divided?

Into two parts. One about Sound, the other about the Modes.

SOUND

What is sound?

It is the ἐμμελυς [2] utterance of the voice: that is, suitable for melody; what the Greeks call φϑογγος.[3]

[1]Little is known about the life of this man. Some musical settings are extant under his name, but his treatise remained unpublished.

[2]Agreeable, in tune.

[3]Boethius, c. 480-524, *De Musica, I,* viii. Sonus igitur est vocis casus ἐμμελυς, id est aptus melo, in unam intensionem. Sonum vero non generalem nunc volumus definire. Sed eum qui Graece dicitur φϑογγος. (Sound, therefore, is the ἐμμελυς or tuneful utterance of the voice on one pitch. But it is not sound in general that I want to define now, but what the Greeks call φϑογγος.) Referred to by Glarean, *Dodecachordon* I, ix, 23.

How many things must be considered in a sound?

Two: the kind of sound, and its affect.

How many kinds of sound are there?

Two kinds: the *unisonus* and the *dispar.*

What is the *unisonus?*

It is uniform sound, without ἀρσις or ϑεσις. So of the six syllables, Ut, Re, Mi, Fa, Sol, La, each one may constitute a *unisonus,* in which there is as yet no reason for ἀρσις or ϑεσις.

What is the *dispar?*

It is a sound stronger or weaker by degrees. For of those six syllables the three lower ones are said to be weak, and the three upper ones are said to be strong. So they call Ut and Fa soft, Re and Sol normal, and Mi and La hard. But Glarean says that there is no reason for that,[4] for there are several songs with Mi and La that are sad and mournful.

How many kinds of *dispar* are there?

Two kinds: continuous and interrupted.

And how many kinds of continuous sound?

Two: the tone and the semitone. For in a progression of six syllables, there is an interval of a tone between one note and the next, except between Mi and Fa, where the interval is called a minor semitone. So the tone and the minor semitone cover the whole compass of music, for they are the elements of all the intervals, and all the different kinds of consonance arise from the different positioning of the semitones. Both intervals are called seconds, for they connect two notes that are next to each other, but the tone is called a perfect second, and the semitone an imperfect second.

What is interrupted sound?

It is sound separated by certain intervals; either διαφωνος, [5] like the *ditonus* or *semiditonus,* or παραφωνος, [6] like the

[4]*Dodecachordon* I, ii, 2.

[5]Discordant.

[6]Harmonious.

diatessaron and *diapente,* or ἀντιφωνος,[7] like the *diapason.*

What is a *ditonus?*

It is a major third, consisting of two tones. There are two kinds: from Ut to Mi, and from Fa to La.

What is a *semiditonus?*

It is a minor third, made up of a tone and a minor semitone. There are two kinds: from Re to Fa, and Mi to Sol.

What is a *diatessaron?*

It is a minor fourth, consisting of two tones and a minor semitone. There are three kinds, depending on the position of the semitone. Either it is in the middle, as in Re Sol; or it is at the top, as in Ut Fa; or at the bottom as in Mi La. Within this fourth stand the Tetrachords. The tritone or major fourth, consisting of three tones, is hard. But besides that, καθολικως [8] each fourth has the same quality.

What is a *diapente?*

It is a major fifth, consisting of three tones and a minor semitone. It is especially pleasant to the ears. There are four kinds, depending upon the position of the semitone: Re La, Mi Mi, Fa Fa and Ut Sol.

What is a *diapason?*

It is a perfect octave, made up of five tones and two minor semitones. As the *diatessaron* uses four letters, and the *diapente* five, so the *diapason* uses all the essential letters, a b c d e f g. It runs through and includes all the notes. Therefore there is an octave between every letter and the next one of the same name. For example, between big A and small a, between big B and small b, between big C and small c, and so on. So there are seven species of *diapason,* from the seven big letters to the seven small ones, and again from the small ones to the double letters.

How is the *diapason* divided?

Into a *diapente* and a *diatessaron;* that is a fifth and a fourth. But there are two kinds of division: the harmonic and the arithmetical.

[7]Concordant.

[8]Generally.

What is the harmonic division?

When the octave has the fifth below the fourth.

And the arithmetical?

When the octave has the fourth below the fifth. That way is more in accordance with the theory of numbers than with harmony, for the fourth below the fifth does not sound pleasant.

What are the intervals called that are greater than an octave?

The διασημματα, or intervals that are greater than an octave, are called the same as those that are smaller.

A	Tone	with an octave is called a	Perfect, or major	ninth
	Semitone		Imperfect, or minor	
	Ditonus		Major	tenth
	Semiditonus		Minor	
	Fourth		Eleventh	
	Fifth		*Disdiapason,* or fifteenth	
	Octave			

The διοδιαπασων, or fifteenth, comprises the entire system of music. Those who go too far outside it are not well thought of.[9] Glarean says that musicians (who are called *symphonetae,* or polyphonic composers) rarely extend the lowest and the highest voices, that is the Bass and the Discant, beyond the διοδιαπασων. But if they do, the intervals are judged as though they were within the octaves.

Who invented this whole system?

Guido of Arezzo, who, according to Mattia Palmieri,[10] lived

[9]In the *Quaestiones physicae* (vii, 142) Freig writes as follows: . . . ultra quem si quis conetur progredi, non iam illa vox genuina, sed coacta factitiaque, atque gannitus magis quam vox videatur. Rursus si altius nitaris eam diprimere, protinus a ratione vocis in screatum quempiam degeneret. (If anyone tries to go beyond it [the disdiapason], the voice does not sound like a real voice, but sounds forced and artifical, like a dog yelping. And if you try to make the voice go lower, it degenerates from its true nature into a kind of croak.)

[10]The great *Chronicon*, a history of the world from its creation, was written by the Italian historian, Matteo Palmieri (1405-1475), but not published until 1483 in Venice. The book was continued by Mattia Palmieri (1423-1483) and further editions were published in 1529 and 1536 at Basel.

under Henry II in the year 1018. Here is his chart.[11]

SCALA GVIDONIS ARETINI
ad paginam 162 referenda.
† † †

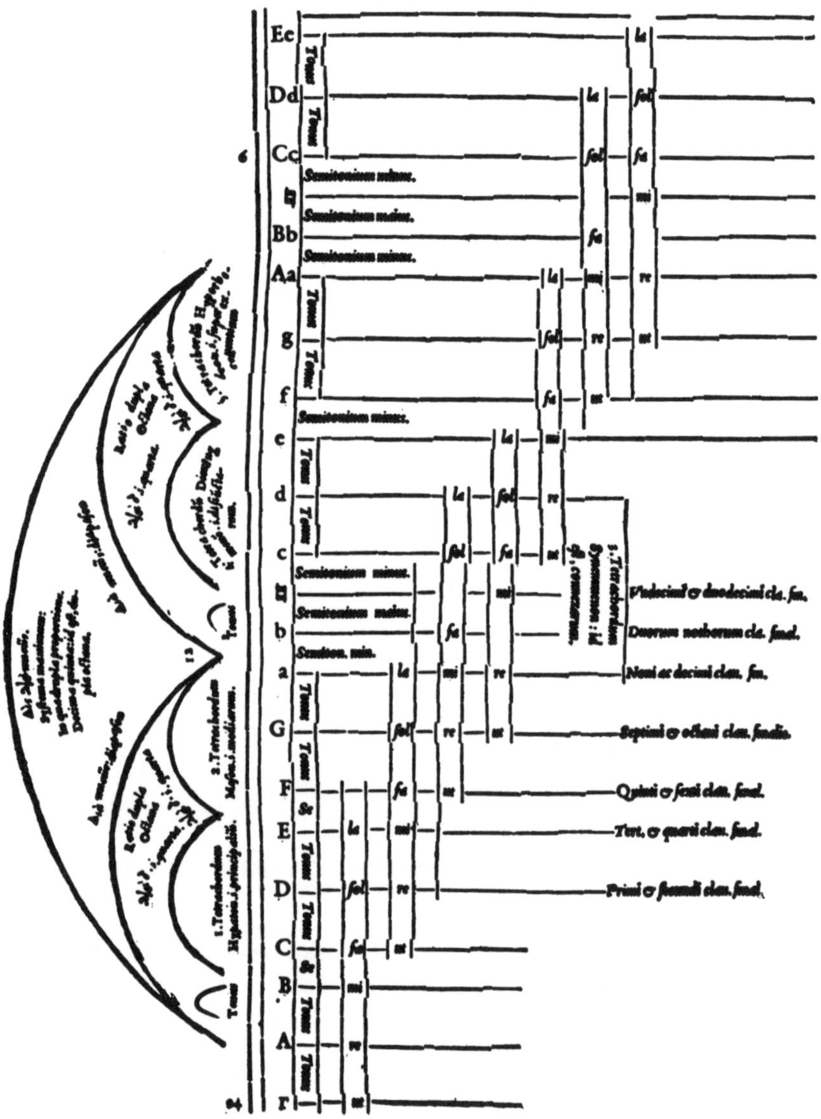

[11]In the original the chart appears as a folding table at the back of the book, with a note explaining that it refers to this page.

What is the order of the notes in this chart of Guido's?

There are two. The one on the left is Greek, the one on the right is Latin.

What does the one on the left contain?

The consonances of the Ancients consisting of four tetrachords, that is the entire system or διοδιαπασων from A re to Aa la mi re, divided into four as the numbers 6 to 24 indicate. In Latin it is called a fifteenth, the middle is a la mi re which divides it into two, with a διαπασων or octave on each side, as the numbers indicate: 12 in the middle, 6 above, and 24 below. Each octave is made up of two tetrachords Mi to La with a tone added on the bottom.

What does the one on the right contain?

The letters of the keys, with the intervals; and the placement or order of the seven notes, to which the *synemmenon* of the tetrachords has been added to avoid confusion.

What is a key?

It is a letter that opens a song, just as a key opens a lock. Hence the metaphor.

How many keys are there?

There are as many keys as there are syllables.[12] But two (which are called "signposts") are usually put in the margins; these are F and C. And in measured or figurative music, g is also used.[13]

What are the intervals?

They are tones and semitones following each other in the right order.

What are the progressions of the syllables?

Seven progressions were established by Guido, in which mutation of the syllables is especially to be observed.

Why was mutation invented?

[12]Sic. This is clearly a mistake. Probably he meant "There are as many keys as there are letters" (from Γ to Ee).

[13]Glarean (I, iv, 6) says that g is used "in suprema cantilenarum compositarum voce" (in the highest voice of composed songs).

So that the notes could ascend by allowing the syllables to exchange function. For one scale was not enough to go up and down through a whole song. And so when the first scale that goes from Γ ut to E la mi was finished, a second could take its place going from mi to la.

In what way does mutation occur?

Sometimes in short steps, sometimes in long.

How does it work in short steps?

When ascending, the higher syllable mutates into a lower, and when descending, the lower mutates into a higher. In keys that have only one syllable there is no mutation; but in those that have two, there are two mutations; and in those that have three, there are six. And in those that have three, you have to look carefully at the key, b fa ♮ mi. For often there are two lower syllables, for instance on g and a; and sometimes there are two higher: as on C sol fa ut and D la sol re. So here the mutation can be easily recognised from the key b fa ♮ mi. For at that point sometimes mi is sung, and sometimes fa.

When can that happen?

When a small b is put on the b key, either in the margin applying to the whole song, or in the middle applying to some particular notes, then fa must be sung at that point. But if there is no sign, them mi must always be sung.

How does it work in long steps?

In octaves, sevenths and sixths there is no mutation, and the syllables are to be sung as they appear on the keys.

But here is an example of what we have spoken about so far. It is from Glarean,[14] and it is in the Hypomixolydian or eighth mode, to which a tone has been added above and below. It lies between D and d and has a fourth above, Sol to Re, and a fifth below, Sol to Ut.

[14]Glarean calls this "vulgatam . . . cantilenam" or a well-known song (I. viii, 22), and says it is useful for beginners, though he criticizes the use of the word "modi" for intervals.

Ter terni ſunt modi, quibus omnis cantilena
contexitur, ſcilicet Vniſonus, Semitonium,
Tonus, Semiditonus, Ditonus, Diateſſaron,
Diapente, Semitonium cum Diapente,
Tonus cum Diapente, ad hos ſonat Diapaſon, ſi
quem
quem delectat pſallere hos modos eſſe cogno-
ſcat. Euouae.

What is the affect of sound?

It is in the mensuration.

What are the things that need to be considered in mensuration?

The length of the notes and the count.

How many kinds of note-lengths are there?

Two kinds. The notes are either longer or shorter than a semibreve (which is what determines the mensuration).

Which are longer than a semibreve?

The brevis, the longa, and the maxima. A brevis is two semibreves, a longa is four, and a maxima eight.

Which are shorter than a semibreve?

The minim, semiminim, fusa, and semifusa. Two minims, four semiminims, eight fusae or sixteen semifusae are equivalent to one semibreve.

How many kinds of count are there?

Two kinds. Duple and triple.

What is duple?

When one semibreve, or two minims come into one count. That is called tempus imperfectum, and the sign is ¢.

What is triple?

When three semibreves or their equivalent are sung in the time of one semibreve. And this is called triple proportion, or tempus perfectum, and the sign is ⊙ or ○. This proportion is twice as fast as that which is normally called triple.

How many kinds of triple proportion are there?

Three kinds: True, sesquialtera, and common.

What is the true kind?

When the greater number contains three times the smaller. When the numbers $\genfrac{}{}{0pt}{}{3}{1}$ $\genfrac{}{}{0pt}{}{6}{2}$ $\genfrac{}{}{0pt}{}{9}{3}$ are put in front of a song, the value of the notes is diminished by three. So that three semibreves take the place of one semibreve, and three breves take the place of one breve.

What is sesquialtera?

When the greater number contains one and a half times the smaller. When the numbers $\genfrac{}{}{0pt}{}{3}{2}$ $\genfrac{}{}{0pt}{}{6}{4}$ $\genfrac{}{}{0pt}{}{9}{6}$ are put in front of a song, the notes are diminished by half their value. And so a semibreve and a minim or three minims take the place of one semibreve, and breve and a semibreve take the place of one breve. This is also called sesquipla and hemiolia. It differs however from true triple because it adds a fraction of a part, whereas true triple is a multiple. True triple proportion makes three semibreves equivalent to one, whereas sesquialtera makes one and a half. So triple proportion is double sesquialtera; notes are sung twice as fast, because two sesquialterae are equivalent to one triple. If you have two sesquialterae, you have one triple.

What is common proportion?

It is like sesquialtera to sesquialtera, as far as the notes are concerned. But with respect to the beat or count it is different, because the beat falls equally on all the syllables in trochiac rhythm, and splendidly, indeed, but with diminution.[15] And it is written in various ways, sometimes with all white notes, sometimes with all black, and sometimes mixed; also sometimes with breves and semibreves, sometimes with semibreves and minims. There are many signs for it: O_3 C_3 $₵_3$ $\overset{o}{3}$

What is *syncope*?

It is the placing of shorter notes amongst the longer ones, which are divided in their turn, and it is used in all parts of a song, but especially in the Discant, and it is pleasing and beautiful.

[15]This passage is rather unclear, as it is a highly condensed version of the explanation by Glarean (*Dodecachordon* III, viii, 205/6) about *diminutio*. The key perhaps lies in one sentence of Glarean that was omitted here: . . . atque hoc quidem . . . diminutionem vocant, non quod notularum aut valor, aut numerus diminuatur, sed quod tactus fiat velocior. (And they call this *diminutio*, not because the value or number of the notes is diminished, but because the beat becomes faster).

THE MODES

What is a mode?

Nothing other than an octave or διαπασων; that is a fifth connected to a fourth. As in grammar the most outstanding treatment is in oratory, and in dialectic in logic, so in music the most outstanding treatment is in the Modes. The Greeks called them νομος και τροπος. In common speech they are incorrectly called Tones. As in syllogism and logic, so in the musical modes, each has its own ellipse, redundancy and inversion. For they do not always fill out their compass; and they often have a note added either above or below; and they are often inverted, which is why they are called plagal, which means oblique or inverted.

How many things are to be considered when discussing the modes?

Two: the different kinds of modes, and their affect.

How many kinds of modes are there?

Two kinds: perfect and imperfect.

What is the imperfect kind?

It is a fourth or a fifth; a tetrachord– διατεσσαρων, or a pentachord–διαπεντε. For once songs were humble and simple, so that they rarely exceeded a fourth or a fifth; but later they began to expand, firstly to a sixth, and then finally to an octave, the true compass of the modes.

How many kinds of tetrachord are there?

Two kinds: the ordinary, and the extraordinary, each one containing the fourth Mi La.

How many ordinary tetrachords are there?

Four, on the left side [of the table] in proper order; and with two connections they fill out two octaves tone by tone. One octave from A re to a la mi re, or from *proslambanomene* to *mesen*; and the other from small a to aa, or from *mesen* to *neten hyperbolaeon.* And so these two octaves constitute the whole body of sounds, the entire system of music, which is commonly called a fifteenth or a double octave, and the Greeks call it the διοδιαπασων; that is twice through all the essential letters of the notes a b c d e f g.

What are those four tetrachords called?

The first is called ὑπατων; it is made up of the principle or lowest notes, from large B to large E. The second is called Μεσων; it is made up of the middle notes from large E to small a. It is called Μεσων because it was in the middle of the ἐνδεκαχορδος or the eleven-stringed lyre. There used to be three tetrachords that were instituted by Timotheus of Miletus [16] (as Boethius says in Book I, Chapter 20)[17], divided amongst the eleven notes: the *hypaton,* the *diezeugmenon* and the *meson* in the middle. Later the *hyperbolaeon* was added. The third is called διεζουγμενων, or disjunct, because it is separated from small a by a tone. It goes from small b to small e. And the fourth is called ὑπερβολαιων, made up of the highest notes, from e to aa.

The Tetrachord	Hypaton is the Bass
	Meson is the Tenor
	Diezeugmenon is the Altus
	Hyperbolaeon is the Discant

What is the extraordinary tetrachord called?

It is called συνημμενων, and contains the connecting notes, because it is connected with small a. It goes from small a to small d. It is not in the true order of the tetrachords on the left of the table, but on the right. And it is not in the essential scale of music. For the fifth and the sixth tone that nowadays finish on F,

[16]Greek musician and poet, c. 446-357 B.C. He was criticized by the Spartans and the Athenians for adding more strings to the lyre. Mentioned also by Glarean in the dedication to the *Dodecachordon.*

[17]Boethius, *De Musica*, I, xx. ... coaptavit chordam. Timotheus vero Milesius undecimum ... tunc ... tria tetrachorda ... But Timotheus of Miletus added an eleventh string ... then [there were] three tetrachords ...

used to finish on C, and all the tones had mi whenever they came to the key for b.[18]

Then why was it introduced?

For three reasons: 1) So that the song can mutate into a different quality, or a different system, from the diezeugmenon tetrachord to the synemmenon, which means from hard to soft. 2) To avoid the tritone, which is not suitable for diatonic music and which would occur between large F and small b, if there were no fa. 3) So that whenever there is a song with many voices, there is a place for raising the Tenor to the key a fourth above so that the system does not change, and so that the Bass can remain within the scale, which is impossible in Dorian and Hypodorian, if ever the Bass descends an octave.

Is that the only place it occurs?

The tetrachord *synemmenon* does not only occur on small a, but also on large A and aa. There is an example in Guido, who adds another *synemmenon* on aa, and there are examples of it occuring in other places, for instance from large A to large D, in the music of the ancient composers.

How many kinds of progressions are there within a tetrachord?

Three kinds: *Diatonicum, Chromaticum* and *Enharmonium.*

What is Diatonicum?

It has two tones, or a *ditonus,* after a minor semitone; for example Mi fa sol la. That is why it is called *diatonicum.* For three tones one after another sound harsh unless you add a semitone either above or below..Two kinds of *Diapente* Mi Mi, and Fa Fa, have three tones one after another but not in one leap, for the former has a semitone added below, and the latter has one added above.

What is *Chromaticum?*

[18]Freig uses "tonus" here for "modus", a practice Glarean deprecates as "tam constanti pertinacique apellatione" (such a stubborn and constant usage), *Dodecachordon* I, xi, 29. Freig himself says that the word is often used, but "parum recte" (incorrectly). See page 20, line 35. And in the *Questiones physicae* he criticizes those who call modes "tones" as acting "barbare" (like barbarians). VII, 139.

It has a minor semitone, a major semitone, and three semitones or a *semiditonus.* Today composers and musicians use it in *syncope.*

What is *Enharmonium*?

It has intervals of a quarter tone, that is, half of a minor semitone, and a *ditonus.* Today nobody uses that kind.

The progressions are
- by *ditonus* and
  - a minor semitone - *Diatonicum.*
  - quarter-tones - *Enharmonicum.*
- by *semiditonus* and a minor semitone and a major semitone - *Chromaticum.*

Give an example of an imperfect mode[19]

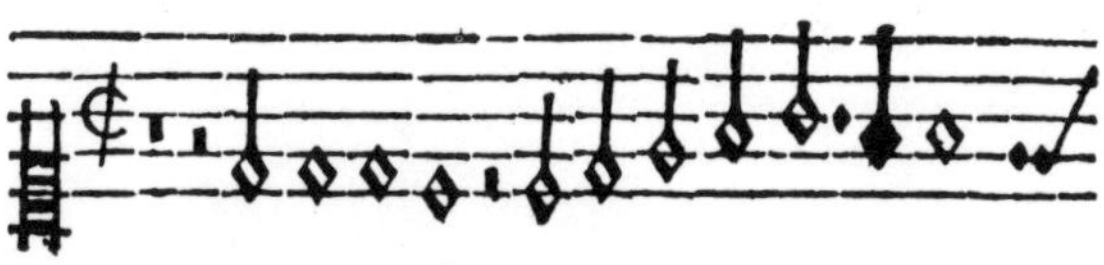

Dont uient cela.

Syncope.

Syncope.

[19]This song, by Claude de Sermisy, first appears in an Attaignant collection published in 1529. See, for this and subsequent songs, Howard Mayer Brown, *Instrumental Music Printed Before 1600: A Bibliography* (Cambridge, Mass., 1965).

Syncope.
Syncope.
Syncope.
Syncope.
Syncope.

The first example ascends, this second example descends.[20]

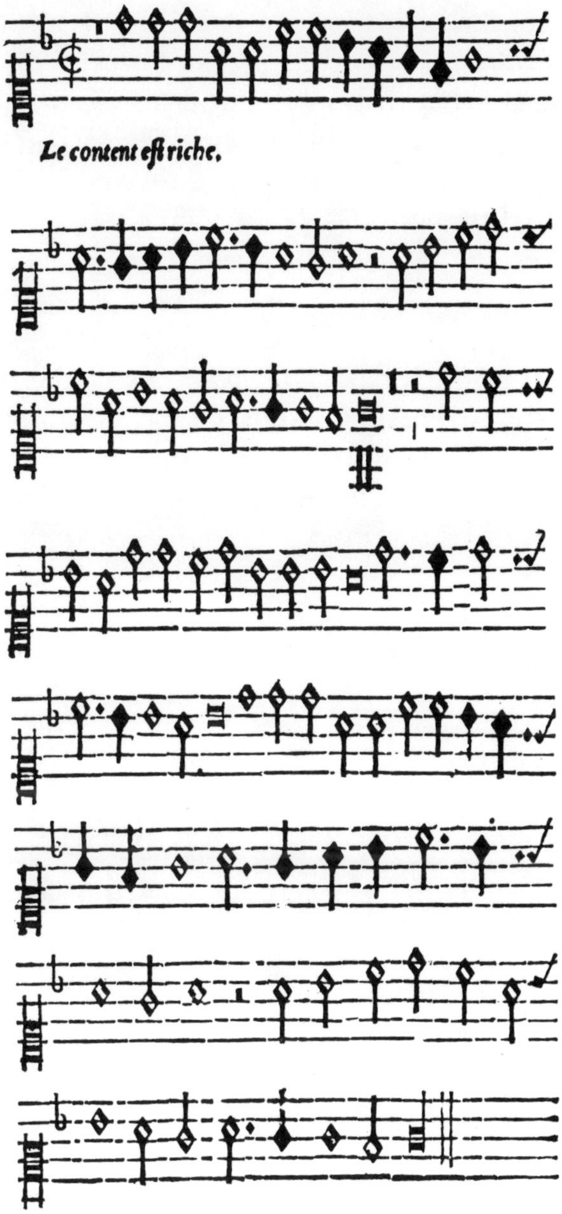

[20]This song, also by Claude de Sermisy, first appears in a 1531 Attaignant collection.

What is a perfect mode?

It is the octave itself, or the *diapason* made up of a *diatessarón* and a *diapente.*

How many modes are there?

Altogether there are fourteen. And they all end on the lowest note of the *diapente* or fifth.

How are they distinguished?

From the seven species of *diapason.* For each of these can be divided two different ways: arithmetically and harmonically; so that fourteen different modes result, as you see here. Each takes its name from the people that made it famous.

Table VII of the kinds of *Diapason,* with the two kinds of division, both arithmetical and harmonic, resulting in fourteen modes. The upper numbers refer to the kind of diapason, the lower numbers refer to the modes.

Scale with hard ♮

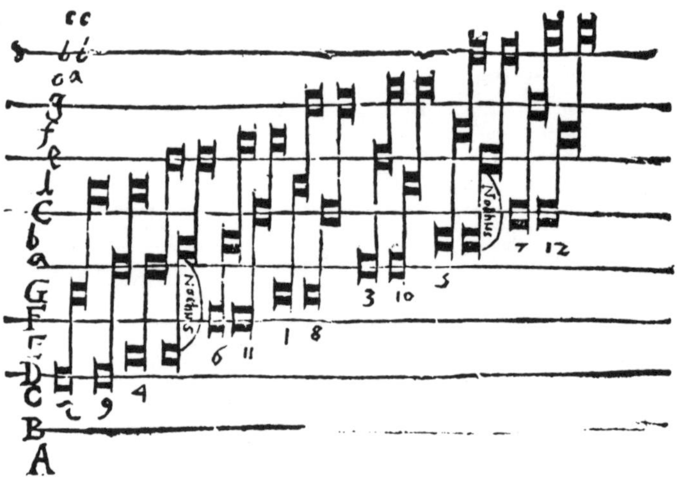

Scale with soft b, in which all the modes have been raised a fourth and transposed to the *synemmenon* tetrachord.

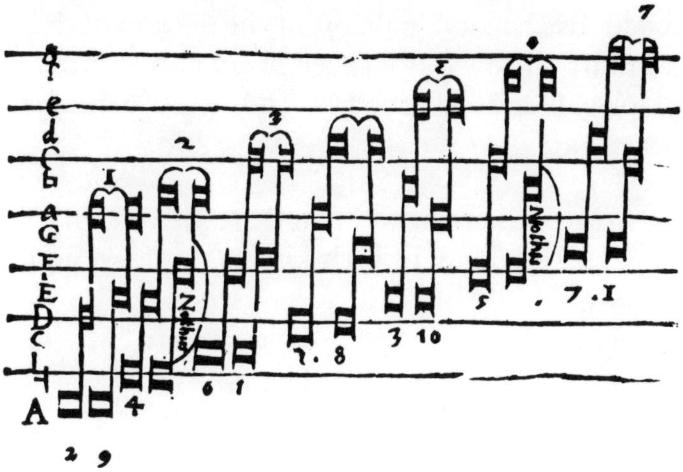

How are the modes divided?

A mode is
- *Simplex*
  - *Legitimus*, γνησιος
    - *Authenter*, or unequal
    - *Plagius*, or equal
  - *Spurius*, νοθος
- *Connexus*, or πλαγιοσυντακτος

What is *Simplex*?

When an authentic or plagal mode is used by itself.

What is γνησιος?

A mode that is properly and neatly divided into a *diapente* and a *diatessaron*.

What is *Authentes*?

A mode that has its final note exactly on the bottom; on the lowest note of the *diapente* or fifth. It is called *authentes* because it is the chief, and the leader.[21]

What is *Plagius*?

A mode that has its final note at the bottom of the fifth, but there is a fourth below it.It is called *plagius* because it is inverted, oblique, plagal and enslaved.[22] And it is named with the preposition ὑπο.

How many authentae and plagii are there?
Altogether there are six of each kind, as you see here:

1.	Dorian	2.	Hypodorian
3.	Phrygian	4.	Hypophrygian
5.	Lydian	6.	Hypolydian
7.	Mixolydian	8.	Hypomixolydian
9.	Aeolian	10.	Hypoaeolian
11.	Ionian	12.	Hypoionian

I. What is the Dorian or first mode?

It is *authentes,* running between D and d, divided harmonically at a, and ending on D. Transposed by a fourth from the *diezeugmenon* or hard tetrachord to the *synemmenon,* it runs between G and g, is divided at d, and ends on G. It was very famous amongst the Greeks, and takes its name from the Dorians. It was praised by Plato in the third book of the *Republic,*[23] and in his *Harmonides,* Lucian[24] calls it **σεμνος,**

[21]The Greek word is αὐθεντης, meaning chief, prince or leader.

[22]See footnote 55.

[23]In the *Republic* Plato gave fullest expression to his ideals of justice and virtue. In the section referred to by Freig, Plato discusses the role of education in the perfect state.

[24]Lucian of Samosata, Greek satirist, c. 120—180 A.D.

which means severe or grave. Apuleius,[25] in the fourth book of the *Florida* calls it warlike. It is most suitable for singing heroic songs and has a wonderful keen gravity. According to Boethius (Book 4) it is the fourth *diapason.*[26]. All modes are known by their beginning, midpoint, and end, and also by their range. The Dorian mode has its range and compass from sol to re or la, and then to re. We shall give an example first in the *diezeugmenon,* then in *synemmenon.* And since Utendal[27] deliberately tried to illustrate the use of the modes,[28] we shall take our first examples from his work, and in the margin we shall note the compass and midpoint of the mode.

Example of the Dorian mode in *diezeugmenon,* which has a tone added both above and below:[29]

[25]Lucius Apuleius, c. 125-? A.D. Best known today for his *The Golden Ass* or *Metamorphoses*; he also wrote the *Florida,* a collection of philosophical comments on a wide variety of subjects, including music.

[26]Op. cit. IV, xiii. Diapason vero consonantiae 7 erunt species, hoc modo: . . . Quarta ab eo quod est L ad D. (There will then be seven consonant types of diapason: . . . The fourth from [D] to [d]).

[27]Alexander Utendal, c. 1530-1581.

[28]Utendal's *Seven Penitential Psalms* (1570) which are liberally quoted by Freig in the *Paedagogus,* are subtitled, . . . ad Dodecachordi modos duodecim aptissima tam vivae voci quam diversis musicorum instrumentorum generibus harmonia accomodati . . . (. . . fitted to the twelve modes of the Dodecachordon, with harmony as suitable for voices as for diverse kinds of musical instruments . . .). Lasso's *Psalmi Davidis poenitentiales* were completed in 1560 but not published until 1584.

[29]A setting of the Nicene Creed, first published in the *Geystliche gesangk Buchleyn,* 1524.

That example ascends, and has a tone added above and below. The next example descends and is in *synemmenon.*

Example of Dorian mode in *synemmenon*
by Georg Forster:[30]

[30]Georg Forster, 1514-1568, editor of the comprehensive collection of polyphonic German secular songs, *Anszug guter alter und neuer teutscher Liedlein* . . . Nurnberg, 1539-1540, which appeared in an expanded second edition in five parts between 1556 and 1565, under a different title: *Ausbund schöner deutscher Liedlein* . . . Many sixteenth-century German composers are represented only in this work. See footnote 49.

The third example is from the first Penitential Psalm by Utendal, in the first part, about the end of the first verse, and beginning of the second, where a fourth follows a fifth. It is in *synemmenon.*

In the second part of the same Psalm, in the first period, there is an octave used more openly, followed by a ninth, that is an octave and a tone, as you can see here:

The fourth example is by Clément Marot.[31] It has a *semiditonus* added below.

[31]Clément Marot, 1496-1544. Best known for translating into French verse and setting to music the Psalms. This song is attributed in most other collections to Sandrin, an early16th-century French composer (dates unknown).

The fifth example has a tone missing below, which is added above. It leaps frequently from re to la.[32]

[32]This appears in a four-part setting by Senfl in Rhaw's 1544 collection *Neue deudsche geistliche Gesenge,* but has also been attributed to Alder.

Quinta.
Tonus assumptus per syncopen.
Sexta
Quinta

II. What is the Hypodorian or second mode?

It is plagal, running between A and a, divided arithmetically and ending on D. When transposed, it runs between D and d, is divided and ends at G. It has a harsh gravity and is not suitable for music of praise. With the Dorian, whose plagal it is, it has in common the fifth re la, but the fourth re sol which the Dorian has above the fifth, this mode has below. The Dorian frequently leaps from re to la, but this mode leaps from re to fa. Its compass is la to re, sol to re. It is the first species of *diapason.*

First example:[33]

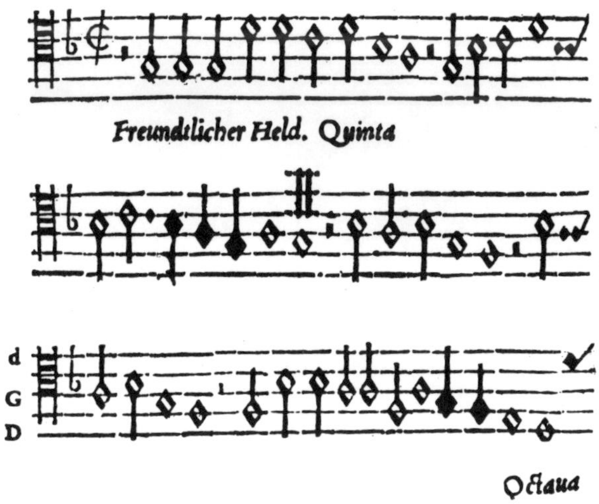

[33]A different setting from the one on p. 71.

Second example:[34]

[34]I have not been able to find this song in Brown (op. cit.) or in any other source.

Third example from Utendal's
Psalm 2, period 2:

III. What is the Phrygian or third mode?

It is authentic, running between E und e, divided harmonically at mi which is ♭ fa or ♮ mi. It ends on E. When transposed it runs between a and aa; it is divided and ends on a.[35] It is an ancient mode and among the most famous. Horace calls it

[35] Sic.

barbarian in Epode 9,[36] as does Athenaeus in book 14 of the *Deipnosophistae*.[37] Lucian in the *Harmonides* calls it ἐνϑεον or impetuous, and Apuleius in the fourth book of the *Florida* calls it religious. It has a certain harsh insolence about it, and easily incites to anger, so that the Greeks called it σκολιος or tortuous. It is the fifth species of *diapason*. Its compass is la to mi, mi to mi.

The first example, which has a *ditonus* added below, is by G. Otmayer:[38]

[36]Lines 5-6. Sonante mixtum tibiis carmen lyra.Hac Dorium, illis barbarum. (The sound of the lyre playing in the Dorian mode mixed with the flutes playing in the Phrygian.)

[37]Athenaeus, fl. c. 200 A. D. The Δειπνοσοφισται is a huge and rambling work covering a variety of topics, including music.

[38]Kaspar Othmayr (1515-1553). He studied with Georg Forster at Heidelberg, and is represented by twenty-six songs in Forster's collection.

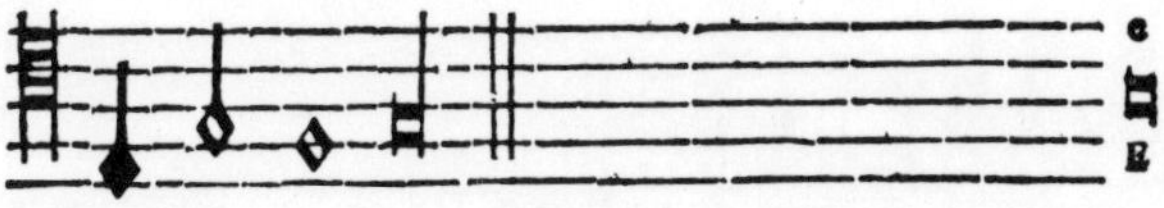

The second example is from Utendal's
Psalm 3, second part,
second period.

In the same Psalm deliberate artifice can be noticed,[39] such as when notes are blackened to signify darkness. This occurs at the end of the second part.

And at the end of the fifth part he uses the same number of notes as there are syllables in the words.

[39]This kind of "Augenmusik" was by this time much in use in Italian madrigals, and relates to a long tradition of musical allegory that reaches back to mediaeval cabbalism and semantics, and forward to the symbolism and rhetorical "figures" of the Baroque.

Finally in the Discant of the same Psalm, in the second period of the last part, when he calls upon our Lord for help, the music wonderfully expresses His descending from heaven to bring aid.

IV. What is the Hypophyrygian or fourth mode?

It is plagal, running between ♭ and ♮, divided arithmetically and ending on E. Transposed, it runs between E and e, divided and ending on a. It is a humble mode, most suitable for tears. For it has a mournful melancholy and suppliant sadness. It is suitable for holy laments, like the Lamentations of Jeremiah. With the Phrygian mode it has the fourth mi to mi in common, but the fifth la to mi is above. It is the second species of *diapason.* Its compass is mi to mi, la to mi.

The example (which has a semitone added above, and a tone added below) is from Utendal's Fourth Psalm, part 3, in the first period.

And the third period of the third part:

In the fourth part at the end of the third and fourth period, the octave of the Hypophrygian is placed more openly. Also the mournful fifth mi to mi is often heard; as you can see here:

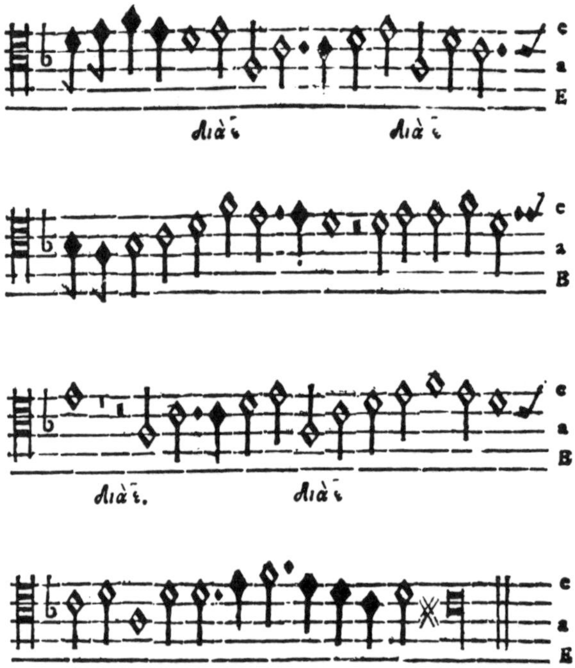

V. What is the Lydian or fifth mode?

It is authentic, running between F and f, divided harmonically at c, and ending on F. When transposed it runs between b and bb, and is divided at F. It is a hard and threatening mode according to Apuleius, and Lucian calls it βακχικος or frenzied. It often has the fifth fa re fa and mi for B, but usually it changes into the Ionian mode which has fa for the b. Moreover the softness of the Ionian is pleasing. It is the sixth species of *diapason.* Its compass is fa ut, fa fa; or fa ut, sol ut when it changes to Ionian — but then it has fa instead of mi.

Example from the beginning of Utendal's Fifth Psalm
when the song descends a fifth after some
intervals of a fourth. It has a
ditonus added above:

In contrast, the beginning of the third part ascends.

In the third period of the fourth part,
the octave is placed more openly.

VI. What is the Hypolydian or sixth mode?

It is plagal, running between C and c, divided arithmetically and ending on F. When transposed it runs between F and f; is divided and ends on b. With the Lydian it has in common the fifth fa fa; but the fourth fa ut is added below. It is the third species of *diapason.* Its compass is fa fa, fa ut; it has mi for b, fa for ♮ but the mi often changes to fa, which turns it into the Hypoionian sol ut, fa ut: just as the Lydian turns into the Ionian.

The beginning of Utendal's 6th Psalm:

VII. What is the Mixolydian or seventh mode?

It is authentic, running between G and g, divided harmonically at d, and ending on G. When transposed it runs between c and cc and is divided at g. It was much used by the Ancients, but in our time it is rare, as is its plagal, since the Ionian carries all before it with its fifth ut sol in the *synemmenon* tetrachord. Musicians often add a fourth ut fa, instead of re sol, above this Ionian fifth. The mode demands it. It often has ut sol, from G to d. It is the seventh species of *diapason.* This is the only mode in which the number of the *diapason* and the number of the mode are the same. As for the rest: the Hypodorian is the first species of *diapason,* but the second mode; the Hypophrygian is the second species of *diapason,* but the fourth mode. The third *diapason* is the sixth mode; the fourth is the first; the fifth is the third; the sixth is the fifth. Only the seventh species of *diapason* is the seventh mode. Its compass is sol re, sol ut.

Ludwig Senfl.[40]

[40]c. 1486—c. 1543. Senfl was of course a fellow countryman of Glarean. There are several laudatory references to him and some examples of his music in the *Dodecachordon.*

The fourth part of Utendal's Seventh Psalm,
at the end of the second period and
beginning of the third and fourth:

VIII. What is the Hypomixolydian or eighth mode?

It is plagal, running between D and d, divided arithmetically and ending on G. When transposed it runs between G and g, is divided and ends at c. It is a completely smooth mode and was considered a great delight by the ancient churchmen. It has a natural pleasantness, which is known to few musicians of our time. It has the same *diapason* as the Dorian, but is divided at a different place. It has the same fifth, ut sol, as the Mixolydian. Its compass is sol ut, sol re. It often has ut fa, from G to c.

How does this eighth mode arise?

There are only seven true modes for the seven species of *diapason.* But this eighth mode arises from the inversion of the fourth *diapason.* It is divided in two ways, arithmetically and harmonically. Four species of *diapason* so far can be neatly divided — the first, the third, the fifth and the seventh; but the remaining two,[41] the second and the third,[42] cannot be neatly divided, because in one part there would be a *semidiapente* instead of a fifth, and in the other a tritone instead of a fourth.

Example from Ludwig Senfl:

[41]Sic.

[42]Sic.

From Utendal's first Prayer.[43]

IX. What is the Aeolian or ninth mode?

It is authentic, running between A and a, divided harmonically and ending on E.[44] When transposed it runs between D and d, and is divided at a. In church music it seems to have been the foremost mode, so that it appears in the Apostles' Creed[45] and the Lord's Prayer. Apuleius calls it a simple mode in Book 4 of the *Florida.* It is adaptable, mild and wonderfully smooth for lyric music. It is commonly called the *modus peregrinus.*[46] It has the same *diapason* as the Hypodorian, and it

[43]These settings are included with the Seven Penitential Psalms: . . . adjunctis ex prophetarum scriptis orationibus . . . 5 . . . (. . . including 5 prayers from the prophets).

[44]It is curious that Freig gives the *finalis* as E, but his example follows the text.

[45]More probably the Nicene Creed.

[46]Glarean says he does not know how it acquired the name. (*Dodecachordon* II, xvii, 108—9.)

is also very similar in nature to the Dorian, with which it has the fifth re la in common. But the fourth is different, with mi la instead of re sol. Its compass is la mi, la re.

Example from Utendal's second Prayer.

X. What is the Hypoaeolian or tenth mode?

It is plagal, running between E and e, divided arithmetically and ending on a. When transposed it runs between a and aa, and is divided at d. It has the same *diapason* as the Phrygian, and the same fifth, re la, and fourth, mi la, as the Aeolian, but the fourth is below. Its compass is la re, la mi.

Example from Utendal's third Prayer,
fourth part:

XI. What is the Ionian or eleventh mode?

It is authentic, running between C and c, divided arithmetically[47] at G, and ending on C, the last note of the fifth, though sometimes it ends on the last note of the fourth. Transposed up a fourth, it runs between F and f and is divided at c. It is named after the Ionian people in Asia Minor (who had twelve city states, as Strabo writes in book 14[48]). It was called γλαφυρος, or pleasant, by Lucian, fickle and wanton by Apuleius. It is most suitable for dances, and trochaic or iambic poems. So it is not in great use in our time. It usually arises from a corruption of the Lydian mode. It is the third species of *diapason.* Its compass is fa ut, sol ut.

Example from the fourth Prayer of Utendal.
A *ditonus* is added above.

[47]Sic.

[48]The Γεωγραφια of Strabo (b. 63 B.C.) was one of the most important works of geography and history in antiquity.

Example in *synemmenon* by
Johann Leonardi of Longenaius:[49]

Another example in *synemmenon* by Georg Forster:

[49]Johann Leonardi, composer, beginning of 16th century, known only from the *Ausbund schöner deutschen Liedlien*,1556-1565. In two sixteenth-century collections this song is attributed to Jacob Meiland (1542-1607).

XII. What is the Hypoionian or twelfth mode?

It is plagal, running between G and g, divided arithmetically and ending on c. When transposed it runs between c and cc, and is divided at f. It is the inversion of the Mixolydian mode, or seventh species of *diapason.* It is in very great use now, though it used to be in exile, together with its authentic counterpart. It is most suitable for calendar songs and love songs. The range of the horn lies within the limits of this mode. But the fifth sol ut sounds in such a way that you could scarcely distinguish it from la re. But the fourth below it, fa ut, is in accordance with sol re. Its compass is sol ut, fa ut.

Example from the fifth Prayer
of Utendal:

g
c
G
Διὰ πασῶν.

Another example:[50]

[50]This appears first in a 1558 collection by Sebastian Ochsenkun, where it is attributed to Steffan Zyrler (dates unknown).

Another example by Georg Forster:

Another example by J.v. Brandt:[51]

Another example by Georg Othmar:[52]

[51]Jobst von Brandt, 1517-1570. A friend of Georg Forster, he is represented by 62 songs in the *Ausbund.* In other collections this song is attributed to Thomas Stolzer (c. 1490-1526).

[52]See footnote 38. Despite the different spellings, it would appear that Kaspar Othmayr is meant in both cases (v. Eitner).

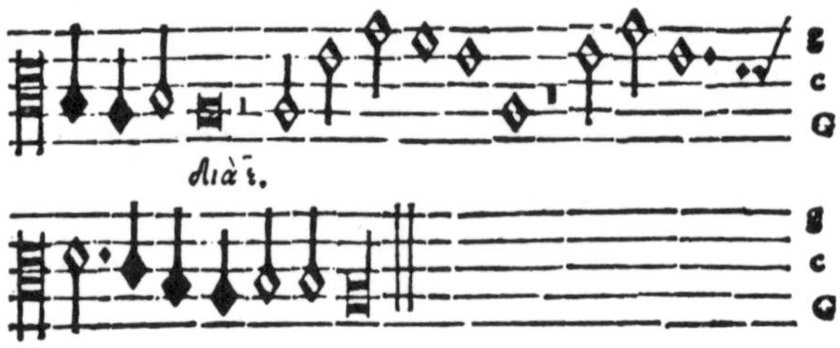

Another example by Georg Othmar:[53]

Another example by Ludwig Senfl:

[53]In two other collections this song is also attributed to Jacob Meiland.

What is the *Nothus* or spurious mode?

It is a mode that cannot be neatly divided into a fifth and a fourth; but only into a tritone and a *semidiapente.*

How many spurious modes are there?

Two: Hyperaeolian and Hyperphrygian.[54]

What is the Hyperaeolian?

It is the authentic *nothus,* running between ♮ and b. It has a *semidiapente* below, and a tritone above. Its name derives from the fact that its position is just above the Aeolian. It is the second species of *diapason.*

What is the Hyperphrygian?

It is the plagal *nothus,* running between F and f. It has the tritone below and the *semidiapente* above. Its name derives from the fact that its position is just above the Phrygian. It is the sixth species of *diapason.* In the same way that the master mode, the Hyperaeolian, is rejected, and was not made famous by any people, taking its name from its position and not from any people's name, so its servant,[55] the Hyperphrygian, is spurned, and has the prefix ὑπερ[56] from its position.

[54]Glarean reluctantly gives examples of both these modes (See *Dodecachordon* II, xviii, 113, and II, xxv, 132, respectively, for monophonic examples, and III, xiv, 276, and III, xxi, 345, respectively, for polyphonic examples).

[55]There is an untranslatable play on words here, when the authentic mode is described as *herus,* leader or master, corresponding to the Greek ἀυθεντης, and the plagal mode accordingly becomes *servus,* servant or slave.

[56] ὑπερ - above

So much for the simple modes. Now let us discuss *connexus.*

What is *connexus*?

It is when a plagal mode is connected to its authentic. Therefore it is called in Greek πλαγιοσυνταϰτος. [57] There is an example in the music for Passion Sunday, where there is a fifth in the middle for the Evangelist. The fourth above is for the Jews and the others; the fourth below for Christ. And so there two modes are connected — the fifth and the sixth, or the Lydian and the Hypolydian. See *Dodecachardon,* Book 3, Chapter 24.[58]

Which fourths and fifths are common to which modes?

The fifth	Re la, is common to the first, second, ninth and tenth modes. Mi mi, is common to the third and fourth modes. Fa fa, is common to the fifth and sixth modes. Ut sol, is common to the seventh, eighth, eleventh and twelfth modes.

These fourths are common to four modes each	Re sol, to the first, second, seventh and eighth. Mi la, to the third, fourth, ninth and tenth. Ut fa, to the fifth, sixth, eleventh and twelfth.

How many affects of the modes are there?

Two: Interchange or ϰρυψις [59] in music and *analogia fugarum.*

What is ϰρυψις in music?

It is when the modes are interchanged. See *Dodecachordon,* Book 2, Chapter 11.[60]

What is *analogia fugarum*?

[57]Connected to the plagal.

[58]Glarean says that this connection is rare since Lydian so often becomes Ionian.

[59]Hiding or concealment.

[60]In this chapter Glarean discusses how some modes can be interchanged smoothly (e.g., Ionian and Hypoionian into Dorian and Hypodorian), whereas other changes (e.g., Dorian to Phrygian) are harsh and unsuitable.

It is the confusion of the species of mode, and it is either continuous or disjunct.[61]

What is continuous?

When all the voices start at the same time.[62]

What is disjunct?

When the Discant follows the Altus, and the Tenor follows the Bass. And it can be the reverse, or it can be interchanged. The reverse is when the Altus follows the Discant, and the Bass follows the Tenor. Interchanged is when the Discant follows the Tenor, and the Altus follows the Bass.

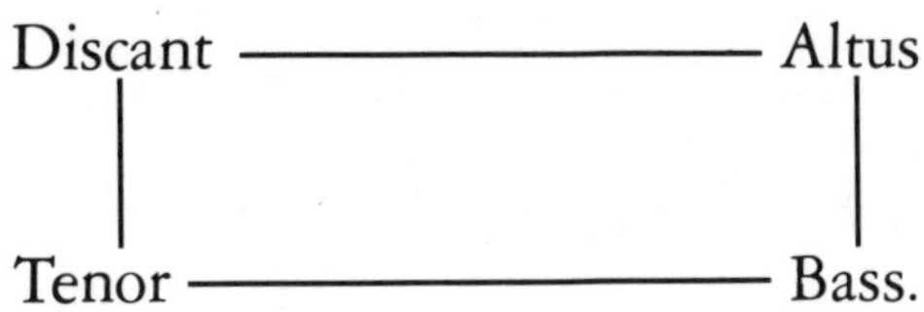

END

[61]This presumably refers to imitative polyphonic writing, when the species of the modes are "confused".

[62]For example in mensuration canons.

HORACE'S FIRST ODE

Book One.[1]

[1]The musical settings of Odes I and III are the same as in Glarean. The melody for Ode II, however, is taken from Glarean's setting of a poem in Sapphic metre by Aurelius Prudentius, an early Christian poet (348-c.410). Setting Horatian Odes to music had become a fairly well-established practice in the sixteenth century. See W. Kirkendale's article *"Franceschina, Girometta, and their Companions"* in *Acta Musicologica* 44 (1972), 191.

Second Ode

Third Ode in the Dorian mode which adds a *semiditonus* above the *diapason.*

Il li ro bur & æs tri plex.
Cir ca pe ctus e rat qui fra gi lem tru ci
Com mi sit pe la go ra tem. Pri mus,
nec ti mu it præ ci pi tem Afri cũ
De cer tan tem Aqui lo ni bus.

APPENDIX I:
INDEX TO COMPOSERS AND UNATTRIBUTED COMPOSITIONS IN THE 'PAEDOGOGUS'.[1]

[1]Where possible the original source for these pieces, and the name of the composer, have been given in the footnotes.

APPENDIX II: WORKS CONSULTED IN SEARCH FOR A TRANSLATION OF THE 'PAEDAGOGUS'

The following is a select bibliography of sources I consulted in an effort to determine whether a translation of Freig's *Paedagogus* had previously been attempted. Perhaps it will prove useful to others conducting a similar search.

A Bibliography of Periodical Literature in Musicology and Allied Fields. Washington, D.C., 1938-43.

Bibliographia Musicologica — A Bibliography of Musical Literature. Utrecht, 1968-.

Bibliographie des Musikschriftums. Leipzig, 1936-.

Chartotheca Translationum Alphabetica. Frankfurt am Main, 1961-72, and 1977.

Index Translationum: Répertoire international des traductions. Paris, 1932-.

Index Translationum: Cumulative Index to English Translations 1948-1968. Boston, 1973.

International Index of Dissertations and Musicological Works in Progress. Ed. Adkins and Dickinson. Philadelphia, 1977. Supplements: *Acta Musicologica* 1978; and Philadelphia, 1979.

"Music Theory in Translation: A Bibliography." Ed. Coover. *Journal of Music Theory* 1959. Supplement 1969.

"Register of Theses on Music." Ed. Doe. Royal Musical Association *Research Chronicle* no. 3, 1963, with amendments and additions up to no. 16.

Thèses de doctorat en langue française relatives à la musique: bibliographie commentée. Ed. Gribenski. New York, 1979.

Verzeichnis deutschsprachiger musikwissenschaftlicher Dissertationen 1861-1960. Ed. Schaal. Musikwissenschaftlicher Arbeiten, no. 19. Kassel, 1963.

BIBLIOGRAPHY

Benzing, Josef. *Die Buchdrucker des 16. und 17. Jahrhunderts im deutschen Sprachgebiet.* Wiesbaden, 1963.

Beurhaus, Friedrich. (Beurhusius) *Erotematum musicae libri duo, ex optimis huius artis scriptoribus .vera perspicuaque methodo descripti. Cum praefatione D. Ioannis Thomae Freigii.* Nürnberg, 1580.

Musicae rudimenta e pleniore eius descriptione, itemque exempla quaedam facilia ad puerilem exercitationem e bonis auctoribus collecta. Dortmund, 1581.

Blume, Friedrich. *Renaissance and Baroque Music: A Comprehensive Survey.* (Translated by M.D. Herter Norton.) New York, 1967.

Syntagma musicologicum: Gesammelte Reden und Schriften. Kassel, 1963.

Blumenbach, Johann Friedrich. *De generis humani varietate nativa.* Göttingen, 1775.

Boccardo, Gerolamo (ed.). *Nuova enciclopedia italiana.* Torino, 1875–88.

Boethius. *Anitii Manlii Severini Boetii . . . opera quae extant omnia.* Basel, 1570.

Brown, Howard Mayer. *Instrumental Music Printed Before 1600: A Bibliography.* Cambridge, Mass., 1965.

Bukofzer, Manfred. "Allegory in Baroque Music." *Journal of the Warburg Institute* 3 (1939–40) : 1.

Carpenter, Nan Cooke. *Music in the Medieval and Renaissance Universities.* Norman, Oklahoma, 1958.

Carter, John, and Muir, Percy H. (eds.). *Printing and the Mind of Man.* London, 1967.

Chevin, M. L'Abbé. *Dictionnaire latin-français des noms propres des lieux.* Paris, 1897. (Reprinted, London, 1964.)

Deschamps, Pierre Charles Ernest. *Dictionnaire de géographie ancienne et moderne.* Paris, 1870.

Dowland, John. *Andreas Ornithoparcus, His Micrologus, or Introduction: Containing the Art of Singing.* London, 1609.

Dressler, Gallus. *Musicae practicae elementa in usum scholae Magdeburgensis edita.* Magdeburg, 1571.

Eitner, Robert. *Biographisch-bibliographisches Quellen-Lexicon der Musiker und Musikgelehrten.* Leipzig, 1900–04.

Fétis, François-Joseph. *Biographie universelle des musiciens et bibliographie générale de la musique.* Brussels, 1835–44.

Freig, Johannes Thomas. (Freigius) *Paedagogus, hoc est libellus ostendens qua ratione prima artium initia pueris quam facillime tradi possint.* Basel, 1582.

P. Rami professio regia, hoc est septem artes liberales in tabulas perpetuas relatae. Basel, 1576.

Quaestiones physicae, in quibus methodus doctrinam physicam legitime docendi describendique rudi minerva descripta est. Basel, 1579.

Fux, Johannes Joseph. *Gradus ad Parnassum, sive manuductio ad compositionem musicae regularem, methodo nova, ac certa, nondum ante tam exacto ordine in lucem edita.* Vienna, 1725.

Galilei, Vincenzo. *Dialogo della musica antica e della moderna.* Florence, 1581.

Gerber, Ernst Ludwig. *Neues historisch-biographisches Lexicon der Tonkünstler.* Reprint. Graz, 1966–77.

Glarean, Heinrich. (Glareanus) *Dodecachordon.* Basel, 1547.

Graves, Frank Pierrepont. *Peter Ramus and the Educational Reformation of the 16th Century.* New York, 1912.

Julian, John. *A Dictionary of Hymnology.* Reprint. New York, 1957.

Kirkendale, Warren. "Franceschina, Girometta, and Their Companions." *Acta Musicologica* 44 (1972):191.

Liliencron, Rochus Wilhelm (ed.). *Allgemeine deutsche Biographie.* Leipzig, 1875–1912.

Livingstone, Ernest. "The Theory and Practice of Protestant School Music As Seen Through the Collection of Abraham Ursinus (c.1600)." Ph.D. dissertation, Eastman School of Music, 1962.

Machiavelli, Niccolò.	*Il Principe.* Rome, 1532.
Morley, Thomas.	*A Plaine and Easie Introduction to Practicall Musicke.* London, 1597.
Nelson, Norman Edward.	*Peter Ramus and the Confusion of Logic, Rhetoric and Poetry.* Ann Arbor, Michigan, 1947.
Ong, Walter J.	*Ramus: Method, and the Decay of Dialogue: From the Art of Discourse to the Art of Reason.* Cambridge, Mass., 1958.
Ornithoparcus, Andreas.	*Musice active micrologus.* Leipzig, 1517.
Pantaleon, Heinrich P.	*Prosopographia heroum atque illustrium virorum totius Germaniae.* Basel, 1565–66.
Pauly, August Friedrich von.	*Real-Encyclopädie der classischen Altertumswissenschaft.* Stuttgart, 1837–58.
Reese, Gustave.	*Fourscore Classics of Music Literature.* New York, 1957.
Riemann, Hugo.	*Musik-Lexicon.* Mainz, 1959–75.
Thoene, Walter.	*Friedrich Beurhaus und seine Musiktraktate.* Cologne, 1959.
Virdung, Sebastian.	*Musica getutscht und auszgezogen.* Basel, 1511.
Zarlino, Gioseffo.	*Le istitutioni harmoniche.* Venice, 1558.